Puppy Training:
From **Day 1 to Adulthood**

How to Make Your Puppy Loving and Obedient

Amy Morford

DEDICATION

I dedicate this book to all the puppies that unknowingly bring joy, laughter, unconditional love, and puppy breath to those around them.

TABLE OF CONTENTS

PUBLISHER'S NOTES

Puppy Training: From Day 1 to Adulthood
By Amy Morford

Amy Morford
DogTrainingPlace.Net

CHAPTER 1: THE RIGHT WAY TO HOUSE TRAIN A PUPPY

Getting a new puppy is exciting, but it comes with a lot of responsibility. A new puppy is like a newborn child, and there is more to raising a good dog than you may imagine.

One necessary task is housetraining a puppy. If you know, how to housetrain a puppy before he or she comes home, you will be far better prepared to handle the process.

There's no denying that some dog breeds are easier to train than others. Find out what you can expect with your breed before bringing your puppy home. This will eliminate un-realistic expectations and frustration when it comes to attention span, learning retention and training techniques.

Training any dog, no matter the type of breed, takes time and effort on your part regardless of how smart your breed is. Housetraining any puppy involves patience, consistency and praise/rewards. It does not matter if you are training a Chihuahua or a Poodle there are practices you can implement to train your puppy successfully as quickly as possible.

Choose a potty command to use for your puppy to associate with going outside and relieving himself. Ask your puppy if he is ready to go outside to "take a break" or "go-potty." Use the same word or phrase every time so he associates the act with the command. When he relieves himself outside, reinforce the behavior with verbal praise. Tell him, "good potty" or "good take a break." Praise him using the command you have chosen.

I recommend purchasing a crate. Crate training a puppy will speed up the housebreaking process and reduce accidents. Dogs will not potty where they sleep. They like keeping their den area clean, so keeping him in a crate will help him get accustomed to "holding it." When you crate your puppy, you need to plan on taking him out every hour (in the early stages) for bathroom breaks, water and play. As your puppy gets bigger, so does his bladder, which will allow you to extend how long he can be left crated.

Be consistent. Take your puppy to the same door to go outside. Take your pup directly to the same area of the yard to relieve him and give your potty command. Do not leave the potty area of the yard until your puppy has relieved himself. In the beginning this will require patience. You might have to take your puppy out on a leash to keep him in the desired area of the yard. Calmly repeat your potty command as many times as necessary. The more consistent you are the quicker your puppy will learn the new behavior.

After your puppy has relieved himself, be lavish with verbal praise and reinforce his good behavior with petting, playing with a favorite toy, or by giving him a doggie treat. You are teaching your puppy that business comes first, and is rewarded with attention and treats.

If you make a trip to the yard and your puppy does not relieve himself, do not be defeated. Do not scold your puppy, but do not reward your pup either. Take your friend back into the house and confine him to his crate or an area where he will not leave your sight. Wait fifteen to thirty minutes and start the process of going outside again. Repeat this until your puppy has relieved himself successfully in the potty area of the yard.

If your puppy is out loose in the house always keep an eye on him. Know where he is and watch him. When your pup is out of your sight, accidents occur. Your puppy will give you signs that he's about to go to the bathroom, and you need to be ready. If accidents happen, remain calm and do not scold or punish your puppy. Raising your voice and punishing your puppy can create stress and anxiety, which can lead to more accidents. Remember that your puppy's undesired behavior of eliminating in the house is ultimately your fault, not his.

If accidents do occur, be sure to clean it up well. Use products designed for removing these types of accidents. They usually have ingredients that will eliminate the smell and will help stop re-occurring accidents. Dogs will typically go back to the same spot to relieve themselves, and they find the spot by smell. So use a good, strong product that pulls the smell up to reduce the chances of a repeat accident.

Consistency is rule number one when housebreaking your new puppy. If more than one person in the house is involved with potty training, be sure that everyone is consistent, doing the same things and using the same commands.

It can take a few weeks to a few months to get your puppy trained to the point where you feel comfortable letting him freely roam the house. The more patient and consistent you are, the faster your puppy will learn the desired behavior of eliminating in the yard instead of the house-no matter what breed of puppy you have.

CHAPTER 2: HOW TO PROPERLY CRATE TRAIN A PUPPY

There are many facets to bringing a puppy into your home. Puppies do not sleep through the night, and they constantly need to eat and use the bathroom. Unlike newborns, puppies can indicate when they need to use the bathroom. It is important to learn and understand the signs so that you will know when they have to go.

Crate training is an invaluable tool that can help keep your puppy safe and secure. Crate training a puppy is the smartest and easiest way to potty train any breed. Some people feel that crate training is a cruel method, but puppies actually prefer the use of the crate. To understand why, you need to understand the origin of dogs. They are den animals, just like wolves. They thrive in a den-like environment. They like to have an enclosed space for sleeping-it makes them feel safe and secure.

Choosing the right size crate for your puppy is an important decision. An appropriate crate will provide your dog with ample room to stand, turn around and lay down. If you choose a crate that is too small, your dog will be cramped and will not enjoy spending time there. If you choose a crate that is too large, your dog may feel insecure and become nervous when he is left alone in it.

What size crate should you choose for a growing puppy? In general, you want to purchase a crate that is intended for the size your puppy is right now. However, since puppies grow quickly, and buying increasingly larger crates can become expensive, you may want to choose a crate that will expand to grow with your dog. Many dog crates come with removable panels that allow you to section off the portion of the crate that your dog will be using at each stage of growth.

How do you know if a crate is too big for your puppy? If there is room for the puppy to sleep and then go to the other side to potty, the crate is too large. You do not want to allow extra space for dogs to relieve themselves. The crate should be sized for sleeping, but not so large that they also can use the bathroom.

Purchasing accessories for your puppy's crate can make your puppy feel more secure and comfortable. A fluffy blanket or mattress pad can be used to line the bottom of the crate. The blanket or padding should cover the entire bottom of the crate so the puppy will understand that the area is for sleeping only. Pet stores sell a variety of options for crate bedding. You can also find special mattress pads that are suited for your specific breed of dog. If a breed is prone to arthritis, firmer pads and orthopedic mattress pads are available.

It is also a great idea to have a chew toy inside the crate. Puppies will often wake up in the middle of the night and grow bored. Having a chew toy such as a rubber ball, rope toy, rawhide or Kong is a great way for them to entertain themselves, exercise their mouths and avoid the temptation of chewing their crate bedding.

Many pet owners choose to only use the crate when the dog is a puppy. Once puppies are properly crate trained and know not to potty inside their crates or homes, their owners remove the crates and no longer use them. Some, however, choose to keep the crate for the dog to sleep in, even after the puppy is potty trained. These are both great choices and neither will affect the dog in a negative way.

Crate training should be a pleasant experience and should never be used for punishment. Crate training is actually more about teaching your puppy that they have a space or a "den" of their own. Allowing your dog to routinely spend time in his crate everyday can eliminate unwanted behaviors such as inappropriate chewing, digging, barking and eliminating in the house.

It's normal for a puppy to feel uncomfortable or anxious in a crate initially. Place your puppy in the crate with a command, like "kennel" or "crate" and give your puppy a small yummy treat. Close the door to the crate and stay within your puppy's view so that they do not feel abandoned.

Introduce the crate slowly, only leaving your puppy in it for a few minutes at a time. As your pup becomes accustomed to the crate, gradually increase the amount of time your puppy spends in the crate. It will not be long before your puppy is comfortable and confident inside of it.

Never remove your puppy from the crate if he is whining or barking. If your pup initially cries or barks, ignore this behavior. Only remove your puppy after he or she has quieted down. It is also important to remain stoic or nonchalant when removing your puppy from the crate. If you act excited about removing your puppy from the crate, your puppy will become excited. Save fun and excitement for playtime outside of the crate.

If your puppy is not eating, playing or being directly supervised, get into the habit of crating him. This will keep him out of trouble and he will more than likely nap. Get into the routine of taking your puppy outside after every nap or after a prolonged period of time in the crate.

Most puppies quickly learn and adapt to routines that involve their crates. Give your puppy ample time to eat, drink, play, exercise and socialize. When you are ready to place your puppy back into the crate, it's a good idea to take him or her back outside and give the opportunity for a bathroom break. A puppy that has been exercised will then be ready for a nap inside his or her crate.

Remember, crate training a puppy should not be stressful for humans or pets. When used properly, crate training is an important tool in raising a puppy.

CHAPTER 3: MAKE YOUR PUPPY STOP BITING AND MOUTHING

It is important to understand that all puppies go through a stage where they need to bite and chew things. They need to work and exercise their mouths especially while teething. This is very similar to a baby getting his or her first set of teeth. Puppies feel a lot of pressure in their mouths while their baby teeth are falling out and their adult teeth are coming in. This pressure is only relieved by chewing and biting on things, and it is a natural instinct.

Give your puppy appropriate things to chew on. If you do not provide him or her with items that are okay to chew, they will find things to chew on. Puppies love to chew on furniture corners, such as the leg of a table. (The wood feels good because it is tough.) Shoes are also popular because a puppy can carry them-and because they are made with different materials, they are fun to chew. If you do not want your puppy to chew on household items and personal belongings, you must provide them with lots of items designed for them to bite and chew.

Look into rubber toys that are absolutely indestructible. A puppy can chew on rubber balls and toys for months and months without causing any damage. Rubber toys are also sold with snack holders. You can purchase snacks to fit inside the rubber toy, and the puppy will chew and chew trying to get to the snack. The great thing about these toys is that the puppy will never be able to reach the snack. They will be completely enthralled with trying to get to reach it.

Another good puppy chew toy is a rope toy. Rope is a hard element that puppies enjoy chewing on. Rope is strong enough to ensure a long-lasting chew toy.

Many treats have been specially manufactured for teething puppies. These treats are made of harder substances (but they're not so hard that they are impossible to digest). Look for treats that will not only feel good to your puppy's mouth but that are also healthy for them.

Bones, rawhides, bully sticks, pig ears, etc. are some other options for puppies to chew on. Beware that some dog breeds do not have the jaw strength to chew on certain bones or pieces of rawhide. They can actually break some puppies' teeth or cut into parts of their mouths. Research your breed or check with your veterinarian before purchasing digestible products for your puppy.

Provide your puppy with plenty of chew toys, and you're much more likely to save prized possessions and family heirlooms that might be tempting to your pup.

Never scold, yell or hit your puppy for chewing. It is not your puppy's fault that YOU left items accessible or left your puppy unattended.

CHAPTER 4: STOP PUPPY WHINING AND HOWLING

Some puppies will whine, bark incessantly, or sometimes emit guttural howls when left alone or placed in a crate or kennel. As annoying as it may be, and painful as it may sound, it's actually completely normal canine behavior. Dogs are pack animals, and to be separated from the pack is frightening for them. Their first instinct is to alert anyone who'll listen that they've been left behind. Some puppies will adjust quickly within a few moments and settle right down. Others, however, will carry on the entire time they're left alone or confined. The thing to bear in mind as you train your puppy to overcome separation or isolation anxiety is that as horrible as it sounds, he's not in pain. The worst thing you could do would be to rush right back in and rescue him.

Never Punish with Isolation

If you're in the process of training your puppy to be crated or kenneled for long periods of time, do not use the crate or kennel for time-out or punishment. The puppy's natural instinct is to hate confinement and isolation, so using the crate or kennel for punishment is adding negative reinforcement. Instead, focus on making his time there as positive as possible. Spend several minutes assuring and praising him before you place him inside. Before you close the door, give the puppy a treat to keep his focus off the closing door. Don't immediately walk off after you close the door. Instead, sit or stand and continue the verbal praise for a few moments. The best time to practice this technique is on a weekend, or when you don't actually have to leave the house.

Make the Directive Clear

The only thing your puppy is certain of as you crate or kennel him is that he's being left behind. He has no idea what is expected of him, and he needs direction from you. As you walk away and he begins to protest, give him a firm "no" and ignore further protests. When he stops protesting, wait a few minutes, then return and praise or reward him. It may take your puppy awhile to quiet down in the beginning, but do not return until he remains silent for at least a few moments. Eventually your puppy will learn that you'll come back when he's quiet.

Dual Training Mode

You're not only conditioning your puppy to accept isolation and confinement, you're also introducing bowel and bladder control. When a puppy's anxiety level is elevated, the urge to urinate is natural. Make sure you've allowed your puppy to relieve itself prior to placing it in confinement.

Combating Boredom

Puppies are full of energy and curiosity. Boredom can lead to incessant whining and even Houdini-like attempts at escape. Left with nothing but the crate or kennel to focus on, a puppy may put all of its energy into resistance. Puppies may also chew on their food and water dishes, spilling the contents everywhere and soaking their bedding. Some owners may opt to feed and give water to their puppies prior to placing them into confinement, and doing so again immediately after the puppy is let out as part of positive reinforcement.

If you opt instead to leave food and water for your puppy, it's recommended that you attach the bowls to the crate or kennel in a manner in which the puppy cannot overturn or move dishes. Add things to the crate or kennel that encourage play, such as chew toys, squeak toys, or attached pull-toys. If your puppy is small and the crate is made of heavy material, you can place a bull-clip onto a chew rope and suspend it from the crate ceiling. As your puppy walks under it, the rope will sway, encouraging tug-of-war.

Training Goes High-Tech

Just how long does your puppy continue to whine and howl after you've left? Does he play with the toys? Does he fight the crate all day long? These questions can plague a loving and concerned owner the entire time away from his or her precious pet. Typically, within a week of positive reinforcement crate or kennel training the puppy will adjust to the new routine and spend his day napping, playing, and entertaining him or herself. To assure yourself that he's just fine, you might want to consider using baby monitors or video surveillance. A simple web-cam placed by the crate or kennel will allow you to peek in during the day, and a baby monitoring system will allow you to listen in.

CHAPTER 5: TEACHING YOUR PUPPY TO COME WHEN CALLED

When your puppy runs towards you, call him.

Puppies come home as cute and sweet little furry balls of joy. Inevitably they start getting a little older and start developing minds of their own. Remember that it's never too early to train your dog. Once you've gotten over the adorable puppy phase, you need to begin training your puppy to listen, be obedient and well-mannered. One of the most important commands a dog can be taught is to come to its owner when it is called.

This can be a tricky command for a puppy to learn-all they want to do is play, chew things and run around. Puppies are very much like children, so their energy is high and their attention spans are short. So you need to be patient. The best time to teach a puppy the "come here" command or any command is to review before they eat or when they are hungry. Always use yummy special treats when training your puppy to give him more incentive to pay attention and listen.

Choose the word or command you want to use. Be consistent with your commands and keep your tone the same each time. Also remember to keep your training sessions short. Always try to end on a positive note. And be patient.

A fool-proof way to begin teaching your puppy to come when called is to use the hallway in your house. Shut all of doors and have a helper hold your puppy at about the half-way point in the hallway. Let your puppy smell the treat in your hand, then walk to the end of the hallway and face your puppy. Make eye contact with your puppy and give your come command while holding the treat out in front of you. Have your helper release your puppy. When your puppy comes to you, reward him with the treat and lots of verbal praise. When teaching new commands to any breed of puppy or dog, there is no such thing as exaggerated praise. Make your puppy feel like he or she is the best puppy in the world.

Gradually extend the distance between you and your puppy in the hallway. When you have mastered the hallway, it's time to move to open areas. Start off close and gradually increase your distance. If your puppy does not come to you in an open area, don't think all is lost. Put a leash on him, give him the come command and bring him towards you (reel him in) using the leash. Don't forget to reward with food and praise. Patience and repetition is key when it comes to training a puppy.

If your puppy is showing signs of boredom, is no longer interested in the treat, or isn't listening, stop your training session. Puppies can become bored quickly, so it's best to train in short 5 to 10-minute sessions multiple times a day in the beginning.

When your puppy understands your command and what is expected of him, you can gradually cut back on rewarding with food. Reward every other time until you are eventually rewarding once every 5 or 6 times that they perform the command successfully. This keeps the puppy hungry for treats and helps to establish you as the alpha leader. Your puppy needs to learn to respect you and obey you because you are the leader of the pack who provides for him.

When you have mastered the "come" command, you can begin mixing in a variety of other commands, depending on your breed and your training goals.

What if your puppy isn't motivated by food? Figure out what stimulates and excites your puppy like a favorite toy or ball. If you can't capture your puppy's attention with something he or she they wants the motivation to listen won't be there, and the lessons won't yield the desired results.

If the "come" command is taught properly, you will be able to call your puppy from anywhere, and your puppy will come a running. This is especially handy when your puppy is outside and you want your puppy to come into the house.

CHAPTER 6: STOP THE JUMPING LITTLE PUPPY

PPS is the best way to train an active puppy. PPS stands for patience, practice and self-control. These attributes are not for the puppy-they are for the puppy's owner! Puppies don't know anything other than how to play, investigate, and chew in order to become familiar with their surroundings. Training a puppy is a commitment that requires patience if the goal is to own a well-behaved pet.

Training time should be short. Puppies tire easily. Commands should be simple for the puppy to follow.

Puppies and dogs generally just want to please their owners. They need to be taught what is expected of them.

Pet owners need to understand that puppies are naturally inclined to jump. (Jump on both things and people.) It is a dog's smelling instinct to be attracted to scents that intrigue them. Puppies begin jumping for several reasons: one reason is to actually get closer to the part of the human body where scent is strongest, but they also jump on people because humans unconsciously train them to do so.

We see our new puppies as cute, cuddly, adorable and precious. Therefore, when they jump up, we pick them up with oohs and aahs. As they become bigger pets, jumping on furniture and people is no longer cute. One technique to stop the behavior requires no eye contact and no talking rules. This technique teaches the puppy to concentrate on its smelling factors to remain calm, rather than relying on its sense of excitement.

The puppy has to be trained to realize that it will be rewarded when it doesn't jump.

When teaching your puppy:

- Don't yell and don't push your puppy down in an aggressive manner.

The first part of training:

- When your puppy is jumping on you, stand upright and wait.
- Don't look at your puppy, and don't let him touch your hands.
- Keep your hands up high, and stand there calmly. Wait patiently and your puppy will stop.

When your puppy stops jumping, immediately look at your puppy, pet him or her, and speak encouragingly and softly, by saying something like "good boy/girl." If this starts excitement and jumping up again (and it will), repeat the steps standing upright. Follow this with a command, like "off" or "sit" and quickly turn your back to your puppy. Say the command(s) again to see if your puppy understood. If not, repeat, repeat, and repeat the exercise again. (This will require patience.) For the first few days your puppy may need constant reminders of what not to do.

It doesn't matter whether you are currently in the house or if you are coming through the door-if your puppy jumps on you, training begins immediately. When entering a room or walking through the open doorway, step back outside or turn around. Go into another room while giving the command, "sit."

But the instant that your puppy does obey your command(s), reward him or her with a tasty treat and an acknowledgment by petting and praising your puppy's obedience. Each time you reward your puppy, he or she associates praise with not jumping, and will adopt the learned behavior.

If your puppy is jumping up to reach your fingers for a food treat, place the treat on the floor or in your puppy's dish.

What about friends and family outside of your household? For this level of training, pet owners should enlist others to help the puppy learn that he or she should not jump up on anyone, not even a child. As long as the dog is a puppy, people will often say, "It's okay if he jumps on me because he is so cute." This is not acceptable when you are training.

Explain that they are not to allow the puppy to jump on them. (Pet owners also need to train their friends and family.)

Get others to also practice the training you have implemented for your puppy, both when they are greeted at the front door and when they enter the room. Yes-the puppy should get another treat when he or she obeys others. Repetition is the answer for everyone.

CHAPTER 7: TRAINING YOUR PUPPY ON A LEASH

Training your puppy to walk with a leash is essential. Unless you live in a rural setting, it is probably illegal for your puppy or dog to roam free. Most communities require dog owners to always keep a dog on a leash when the dog is in public. A leash-trained puppy will be a happier and safer puppy. You and your neighbors will be happier. Teaching a puppy how to walk with a leash isn't rocket science. It does however require discipline, patience, commitment, and a little bit of strategy.

The basic thing to remember is that you have to help your puppy get used to being restricted by a leash. A puppy's natural instinct is to go anywhere and do anything he wants. The world is full of sights, smells, tastes, and innumerable objects that can captivate a puppy's attention. He is obviously inclined to explore everything that peaks his interests. Being on a leash, in reality, means submitting to the will of his master or whoever holds the leash.

Some dog owners feel guilty about restricting their dog's mobility. In the long run, however, a leash-trained dog will be more content and easier to deal with. A leash-trained puppy learns to obey his master. You may be able to eventually let him walk in appropriate places without the leash, without the fear that he will run away.

He is not only learning to walk with a leash, he is also learning to be obedient. An obedient dog responds to his owner's commands regardless of whether they are attached to a leash. Dogs are pack animals. Their natural instinct is to follow the pack leader. Teaching your puppy to walk with a leash is exerting your authority and showing him that you are the pack leader.

The Essential Steps

The Collar

The first step in teaching a puppy to walk with a leash is to help him become accustomed to wearing a collar. Although all puppies have their own unique personalities, almost all puppies dislike having a collar placed on them. It is easier to put a collar on while a puppy is distracted doing something else, such as playing or eating. Your puppy will let you know that he doesn't enjoy wearing his new collar. Resist the urge to remove it. Your puppy will get used to the collar after a few days.

The Leash

Teaching your puppy to get used to the leash is a two-stage process. The first stage entails helping him become accustomed to the leash itself. Attach the leash to his collar and let him drag the leash around the house. The second stage involves asserting control over the leash. The puppy then begins to learn that his freedom of movement is being curtailed. Start with small steps. Pick up the leash and tell him to stop. Drop the leash after five or ten seconds and let him have his freedom back. Repeat the process several times over a two to three-day period. He will gradually adjust to the leash. Some breeds are more resistant to leash training than others. It may take a little more time and patience if you have a stubborn dog. Nevertheless, your puppy will eventually become accustomed to his leash if you stay focused and committed.

Indoors

Puppies and first-time dog owners need to learn how to walk with a leash. Practice makes perfect. Keep in mind that you are the leader. Your puppy will follow his natural instinct to go where he wants to go. Practicing indoors with a leash is important *before* venturing outdoors with the leash.

Lead the puppy around the house. Stay firm but don't pull him. The goal is to keep the leash loose. He should walk by your side or slightly in front of you. Keep a little slack in the leash. If the leash is tight, the puppy is exerting his authority over yours. Puppies learn behavior through positive reinforcement. Reward his good behavior with his favorite treat or toy and with words of praise and encouragement.

Outdoors

Once he has learned the basics, it is time to move it outdoors. Choose a path that is easy and free of distractions (like other dogs and so on). Assert your authority. Stop walking and command your puppy to stop if he is pulling the leash. He needs to learn that pulling the leash is a fruitless endeavor. He also needs to learn to respond to voice commands. In other words, don't yank or pull on the leash to change his direction. Tell him to come with you as you change direction. Reward him with a treat when he obeys your command, practice stopping and starting. Command him to sit (if he knows how to sit) when you reach a street corner. Make him wait on your command before you cross the street. Give him another treat and praise him for his good behavior.

CHAPTER 8: TRAINING YOUR PUPPY TO STOP BARKING

One of the most common problems with a puppy in new surroundings is barking. It's natural, but barking can be very irritating to you and your neighbors. Puppies and dogs bark for a variety of reasons: trying to communicate boredom, fear, hunger, thirst, anxiety, etc. Completely eliminating a dog's barking is not always feasible, but the barking can be greatly reduced and brought under control.

The first thing you need to identify is why your puppy is barking. Is it a constant behavior, or is it only brought on by certain events? Your puppy could be barking because of another dog, a cat, strangers at the door, or even because it's lonely and bored. Knowing why your dog barks will allow you to specifically target the problem.

Is the Puppy Lonely and Bored?

One of the more common reasons puppies bark is because they're lonely. Like children, puppies need attention and many times owners can't give the attention needed during the puppy years. Sometimes they outgrow the barking and other times it can become a habit, so it's a good idea to nip it in the bud before it does.

You need to provide your puppy with plenty of items to play with and chew on to prevent boredom. Your puppy must learn to play on its own. Well-intended owners who constantly entertain their dogs have dogs that quickly become lonely and bored anytime they are left alone. When you do leave your dog alone, be sure that the essentials are taken care of. Plenty of food and water are obvious, but play toys, chew toys, rawhides, bones, etc. are necessary, too.

Owners often unknowingly reward their puppies' unmerited barking. If your puppy is outside barking because you are inside, letting your puppy in to quiet him down has just sent the message that barking leads to what he wants. When your puppy barks for no reason, ignore the barking and lavishly reward and praise your puppy when the barking has *stopped*.

Exercise

One way to use up puppies' excess energy is to make sure they have enough exercise. A puppy that has had plenty of chances to play doesn't have the energy to bark excessively at nothing.

How much exercise is enough? The breed of puppy, its size, temperament, and energy level have to be taken into account.

Noise

Leaving the radio or television on when you're away from home is a way to calm your puppy. Studies have shown that the noise of a fan is relaxing to some dogs. You'll have to experiment to see what sounds calm your puppy's nerves.

Obedience Training

Dogs are impressionable, and as puppies they can easily be trained to stop barking with the use of hand commands.

Obedience training is all about repetition and commands. Hand signals and voice commands are commonly used in this type of training. The owner is taught how to train his or her dog so that the dog focuses on the owner and not on what triggers them to bark. It's a bit like desensitization.

Change does not happen overnight, it can take months to properly train a puppy not to bark.

"Speak" and "Quiet"

Training a dog to bark is the first step in training them not to bark.

The words "speak and quiet" are the two words used in training. As you go through the exercise, gently put your hand around your dog's mouth when you say "quiet," and then do the opposite when you say, "speak." This will require lots of repetition and plenty of patience.

Once your puppy starts to get the idea, introduce treats as a reward for obeying your commands. As your puppy learns more, replace the treats with a positive tone when they do well (or a negative tone when they don't do well). As training becomes more advanced you can use hand signals. Pointing the palm of your hand at your puppy will come to mean "stop." Showing your puppy the back of your hand while pulling your hand toward you means "start."

These hand signals are advanced training techniques-you may want to wait until your puppy matures to teach him or her this method.

Bark Collar

Bark collars are popular because they are automated. Bark collars are programmed to emit noise, blast air, or to use electric stimulation. They are designed to interrupt the behavior.

The three variations of these collars work equally-well; it all depends on what you feel comfortable with. Puppies can be ultra-sensitive to electric pulses, so this may not be the preferred collar for a young pup.

Socialized Training

Dogs learn from other dogs, and puppies learn from older dogs. Some puppies are naturally dominant, and that is one reason why they may tend to bark. But they can be trained not to bark by being around other well-trained dogs.

You will need to meet up with another person who has a well-trained dog; or, find a professional trainer you can work with. The first step is to get an overview of how the process works. To learn the signals and commands, you will watch the other dog for a while. Soon your puppy will start to participate in the training exercise along with the other dog.

Most puppies are always in play mode, so it usually takes a little time for them to get the idea. Once they see that the elder dog won't play, the puppy usually starts to imitate the elder's actions and starts to conform to the training process. At this point you can begin to teach the basics like sit and stay. Once your puppy is in "training mode," you can begin teaching him or her speak and quiet.

If your puppy is barking out of dominance, then socializing should teach him or her to interact better with other dogs. This means that your puppy will quickly find out it isn't that tough. The barking will subside once your puppy realizes that it only leads to trouble.

The keywords here are training and obedience. To administer the proper solution you must first determine the cause. Puppies naturally bark, but if the reason is for attention due to being alone for long periods of time, then the solution may not be totally training based.

Shouting or hollering at your puppy is not advised due to the fact that it may encourage barking. Spanking is another no-no. It may achieve short-term results but in the long run your puppy will not be trained-your puppy will be reacting out of fear. No professional trainer will ever advise this as a method to stop your puppy from barking.

CHAPTER 9: STOP EXCITED PUPPY URINATION

The excitement of being introduced to a new environment can result in urination for some puppies. Urination issues need to be addressed immediately. Training a puppy not to pee until they get to a pad, to paper, or outside should be the focus from the first day the puppy arrives home.

Decide What the Root of the Problem Is

Puppies often get excited by people coming home from work, children coming home from school, guests coming over for a visit, and other times when they are greeted. Puppies generally receive an enormous amount of attention whenever they are greeted, and they love it! A puppy tends to get so overwhelmed with excitement that he urinates accidentally. There is also play-time. A puppy that tends to be very active is so consumed with the action of play that he may urinate because of it. Puppies are still in the developmental stages and may not be able to hold urine for long.

Try To Solve the Problem

If a puppy is excited and urinates during greetings from others, try to tone the greeting down. Place your puppy in a comfortable pet crate or carrier. Try not to give too much attention to your puppy whenever you come home. Your puppy will eventually get into the routine of low-key excitement. Another way to keep your puppy from becoming overwhelmed by greetings is to ask guests not to pay attention to your puppy when they arrive.

You can also take puppy outside to urinate whenever someone comes in. The focus then will not be on the greeting, but on potty time.

If a puppy is excited and urinates during active play-time, move play time to outside play only. (This may require you to spend a lot more time outside) The puppy can be limited to small play indoors and this will discourage the pattern of urination.

Walking Puppy Is a Must

Every dog needs to take frequent walks outdoors. The puppy needs to walk briskly and quickly at times. The excitement puppies have comes from the active nature of their being. Exercise is important for the health of your puppy and also increases strength. Frequent walks will also help manage the urge to urinate.

Offer Behavioral Treats

A puppy loves to be praised and rewarded. Do not reward or praise a puppy for urinating when he is excited. Only give treats and praise when your puppy urinates outside. Some people prefer to use clickers and special training tools. The important thing to keep in mind is to reward and praise when the puppy urinates outside. Calm behavior should be rewarded, not excited behavior.

Be Certain There are No Medical Issues

If you try the above tips and find that your puppy is still having issues with urination, consult a veterinarian. Your puppy could possibly have underlying medical issues. Some puppies have health issues that cause them to urinate whenever they are excited. Until the medical problems are corrected, no form of training will work to correct the problem.

Pads, Papers, or Outside

Many new puppy owners prefer to use pee pads or newspapers when training a new puppy. Some people prefer to take the puppy outside to urinate. Whatever you decide to use isn't as important as the consistency in what you are using. Keep in mind that once you begin potty training your puppy, you must follow through with the routine until they are urinating in the correct places.

CHAPTER 10: WHY SOCIALIZE A PUPPY

There are many reasons to socialize a puppy, and the socialization process should take place while they are still young. It is best to socialize the puppy before it is a year old. Puppies that are well socialized will grow into confident, well-rounded adult dogs with a good temperament. The way to socialize a puppy is to expose it to as many dogs, people, places, sights and sounds as possible. In doing this, the puppy is learning to experience and adapt to new situations and to not be fearful.

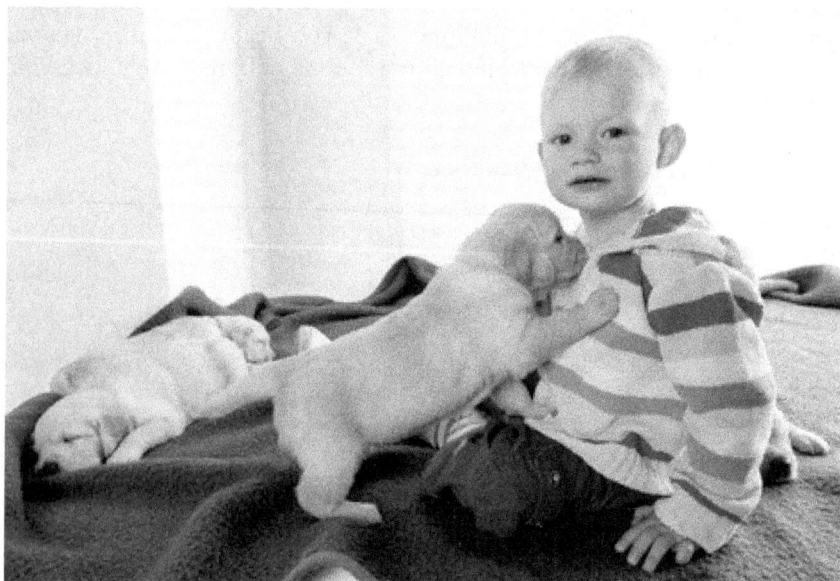

They will be less likely to be aggressive towards other dogs and strangers if they have been exposed to them before the age of one. Puppies that are not socialized often grow into the types of dogs that an owner has to get rid of. Sometimes owners don't realize what a danger their unsocial dog has become until after the dog has mauled or maimed someone. Adult dogs that miss the window of opportunity to be socialized properly have a greater chance of attacking other dogs or people. This is unfortunate but true.

Dogs that were not exposed to many different people when they were pups have the tendency to become aggressive adult dogs. This is especially true for breeds with aggressive temperaments like pit bulls and chows. Dogs that were socialized as puppies and exposed to many different interactions with humans have a tendency to be friendlier adult dogs that don't attack or turn on humans.

It is also important for dogs to get along with other dogs and learn the social cues needed to get along with other dogs. When puppies are allowed to have interactions with many different dogs, they grow up learning not to be afraid or to be too dominant when they grow up. Dogs are pack animals and need to learn how to be submissive to dominant cues given by other dogs.

It is the owner's responsibility to shape his or her puppy into a healthy adult dog by providing the pup with chances to be socialized properly. The owner needs to visit parks and conduct play dates with other dogs, to place them in situations or events with other dogs, to have the puppy attend dog behavior or obedience classes, or to put them in a good doggy daycare. By exposing the puppy to different situations, the puppy can learn proper behaviors that are expected and learn not to fear interactions with other dogs.

In order to socialize a puppy to interact well with human beings, an owner must expose the puppy to many different people and different situations in order to eliminate fear and aggression at an early age. Exposing the puppy to children is also extremely important. Dogs who were never around children as puppies may not act predictably around children, and this can be dangerous. Children are loud, hyper, and some dogs are fearful of this behavior, especially when they've never been socialized to accept this type of interaction. A dog that hasn't been properly socialized could very easily attack or bite a child.

It is important during the socialization process that the owner lets the puppy know what behaviors are acceptable. If a puppy shows aggression toward other dogs or humans, then it should be corrected. The dog should be put in the same situation over and over again until it learns how it is expected to behave.

Dogs who were raised on a chain in the backyard and are never given the chance to be around humans and other animals at a young age will not know how to react when put in an unfamiliar situation. If that dog were to escape or come in contact with a human, the dog would most likely view the human as an intruder and act aggressively. This can turn into a disastrous situation. Dogs need love and affection in order to grow into decent dogs. A dog that is never allowed to socialize with humans and is neglected is the most dangerous type of dog. These dogs shouldn't be trusted because they will exhibit unpredictable, potentially aggressive behaviors.

It cannot be stressed enough-socializing a puppy is the most important thing an owner can do to help his or her puppy grow into a well behaved dog.

CHAPTER 11: GETTING YOUR PUPPY TO STOP CHEWING

There are many reasons why puppies chew, but mostly it is to explore their world. Just like human children, puppies put things in their mouths to learn about the world around them. It is important that you as a puppy owner realize that chewing is a natural action for all dogs, and you should not attempt to stop it completely. However, you should help your puppy learn what items are okay for it to chew on and what items are not. If your dog is chewing things it should not be chewing, there are several things that you can do to help stop the destruction of valued items.

Put your things away. In many ways, puppies are just like toddlers in that if an item is within easy reach, the pup will chew on it. Make sure that items like shoes, trash, books, glasses and remotes aren't within easy reach.

Leaving your things all over the place is an unspoken invitation for your dog to chew on whatever he likes.

Give your puppy toys and treats. Boredom is a major reason puppies chew. To keep your puppy from destroying household items out of boredom make sure the pup has plenty of toys. Squeaky toys seem to be the best option. The noise they make distracts your puppy from other non-vocal items.

Treats, particularly edible bones, are a great way to let your puppy chew without sacrificing your belongings. Edible bones are great training aides. If you catch your puppy chewing on something it shouldn't, firmly say, "no" while removing the item. Immediately replace your chewed item with a puppy-approved item such as a toy or an edible bone. Your puppy will learn over time that their toys and bones are okay to chew on and your things are not.

You should never discipline your puppy when you discover a chewed item. The puppy will not make the association between the punishment and the chewed item. You should only correct your puppy if you catch the puppy chewing at that moment, otherwise you'll confuse and scare the dog, which makes the correction pointless.

Make sure you supervise your puppy properly. It isn't wise to allow your puppy to roam the house unsupervised. Like toddlers, if your puppy is quiet and isn't in your line of vision, something is amiss. Keeping an eye on your puppy while you are at home is important. The older your puppy gets and the more toys the puppy has, the less likely the pup will be to chew on things that shouldn't be chewed on.

When you aren't able to keep an eye your puppy, try to find a place that you can dog-proof. A baby gate and playpen are great tools to help keep your puppy out of trouble. I highly recommend that you crate train your puppy so that the pup has a safe and secure place to spend time and chew on toys while you aren't home. It is also peace of mind for you because it allows you to leave your puppy without worry that there will be trouble or destruction when you're gone.

It's important to understand that boredom leads to destructive behaviors like chewing. The simple fact is that your puppy won't know how to behave if you don't teach him what is and isn't acceptable behavior. Puppies can't learn what they're not taught.

To minimize boredom, make sure you give your puppy plenty of mental and physical exercise. Always remember as a pet owner that a tired dog is a good dog. To understand how much exercise your puppy needs you can always research his breed. Different breeds like different activities and have different exercise needs. If you have a mixed breed puppy, start at about one hour of exercise a day depending your pups size and energy level.

CHAPTER 12: CALMING DOWN YOUR PUPPY

The feeling of joy that comes from having a new pet can soon turn to anxiety if your new puppy has a hard time adapting to his new environment. Usually when you bring home a puppy, it is its first separation from its mother and littermates. This is a stressful event in the life of a young dog. Then you add to that the extra stress of entering a new home where new, strange people are very excited to see him. No wonder most puppies are anxious. You don't want your first few months with your new pet to be overly stressful. There are several ways to help your new pet relax and adapt to his new home.

Prevention is the Best Cure

You can save yourself a lot of trouble and save your new pet a lot of stress if you make an effort to keep your pet out of overly stressful situations. Many puppies find an area with loud noises or excessive activity to be stressful. This is especially true of places where there are children.

Children are unpredictable and loud. Places such as schools, playgrounds and parks are a no-no for many puppies. You may think a few minutes out at the local park will not be that big of a deal, but in the end you could spend hours trying to calm your new puppy down. This just isn't worth the trouble in the early days of your relationship. You are literally your puppy's new parent. It is your responsibility to keep him out of situations that he will find stressful or frightening, just as you would with a child.

T-Touch Massage

Many pet owners are discovering the amazing benefits of pet massage. T-Touch is a Swedish form of skin massage. This is not like a deep muscle massage that you would get at a spa. Rather, T-Touch, is a very gentle massaging of just the skin in slow, circular motions. Your puppy may resist this type of therapy at first. You should attempt to practice T-Touch for about 20 minutes during your first few sessions. Keep your puppy as still as possible, while gently massaging from his head to his tail. As your puppy becomes more accustomed to this type of therapy you can decrease the time it will take to use the massage effectively. Eventually you should be able to calm your puppy within 5 to 10 minutes.

Kong

A Kong is a wonderful pet invention that can basically be used as a puppy pacifier. The Kong is a toy that can be stuffed with food that the puppy enjoys. Once you know what type of food to stuff it with, you can freeze the Kong. During stressful situations, give the Kong to the puppy. He will wrestle and play with the Kong as the snack defrosts. The snack is wrestled out a little at a time, keeping your pup occupied for up to an hour. Usually, your puppy will grow tired and be ready for a nice snooze.

Herbal Help

There are also holistic products on the market that can help you calm your puppy. These products use a combination of essential oils, such as lavender, and synthetic pheromones that are similar to those emitted by a mother dog. These products can be sprayed near an anxious puppy and will elicit calming effects when inhaled.

Early Training

Never assume that it is too early to get your puppy in a good routine. Puppies, like little children, thrive on routine. When a puppy knows what to expect there is less to be anxious about. From day one, establish a regular feeding, playtime and sleep routine. It is also important for the puppy to have a regular area for each of these activities. Establish a definite feeding area, sleeping area and play area. After a few weeks, the puppy will come to recognize what activities will be taking place in each location. Also, you can begin to gently introduce some basic commands. This will help the dog to understand that there are some boundaries. Boundaries are comforting to young animals and will add to his sense of calm.

Check Yourself

Often our pets will mirror our own behaviors. If you are anxious or the dog is in an environment surrounded by much anxiety, he may begin to mirror those emotions in his own behavior. Checking your emotions and anxiety can have a huge impact on the attitude on your new puppy. If his environment is too exciting or loud, it is your job to make whatever adjustments are needed to ensure your puppy's emotional well-being.

A calm and happy owner in a calm and happy environment will have a calm and happy dog.

CHAPTER 13: A HAPPY PUPPY IS A GOOD PUPPY

There are always unexpected things that pop up after you bring a new puppy home. We are so anxious to bring an addition to our families and when we do, we suddenly are faced with the equivalent of raising a small child. At times it can be frustrating and challenging. You may even find yourself questioning your decision (and your sanity) when bringing home a new puppy.

On the other hand, a new home with strangers can be overwhelming and a frightening experience for a puppy. Add in other pets and children and some puppies may experience stimulation overload.

New owners need to realize that a puppy will need some time to adjust to its new surroundings. The adjustment period for each dog varies and may take anywhere from a few days to a few weeks or longer.

During your puppy's adjustment period, give lots of love and attention to ease fear or anxiety. Don't force interaction with other pets or children. Some puppies are naturally outgoing and curious while others or more reserved and cautious.

When introducing your new puppy to new things or new people keep interactions low-key, positive, and filled with lots of treats and praise.

The needs of a puppy are really no different than those of us human animals. We all get lonely and need attention now and then. We all need to play and cut loose and we all benefit from positive words of encouragement. We also want to know what is expected of us. We want to fit in and belong, and we all seek unconditional love.

Raising a happy puppy involves more than the basic essentials and some basic obedience. A happy puppy is a good puppy because it is loved, properly socialized, well-mannered, well cared for, has boundaries, and understand their place within the family dynamics.

Happy puppies are treated as a valued member of the family. They are included in daily routines and feel they are contributing members of their packs.

Spend time and energy creating a happy puppy. A happy, good puppy will evolve into a happy and good dog.

CHAPTER 14: WHEN TO PUNISH AND WHEN NOT TO PUNISH YOUR PUPPY

Puppies can bring a lot of joy into its owner's life, but in order to enjoy a long and happy life with a dog, pet owners need to know some basic training techniques. One of the most difficult things for new puppy owners to figure out is when to punish and when not to punish a puppy. Dog owners also must decide on the type of punishment they will use when they do need to discipline their puppies.

Types of Punishment

Using a word like, "no" or "stop" may work for some as a signal that punishment may follow. Although some dog owners believe physical punishment (like hitting a dog with a rolled-up newspaper) is necessary, it is an outdated method and there are other ways to punish a dog. One way to punish a dog is to spray him or her with a water bottle while using the word "no" or "stop". Another way is to isolate him or her for a short period of time after an undesirable action. For example, if your puppy jumps onto the sofa, saying "no" and placing your puppy in a crate or small isolated area for a few minutes will send the message that the particular behavior is unacceptable. If you are using the isolation method for punishment, it is important to not have toys or other rewards present in the isolation area.

In addition to deciding on punishment, it is also necessary to decide which members of the household will be permitted to punish the dog. If multiple family members will be disciplining and training, the same commands and actions should be used by all family members to avoid the puppy confusion.

When to Punish a Puppy

Puppies should be punished when their actions could harm them or someone else. Biting, running into the street, jumping on people, or getting into the garbage can are all examples of actions that could bring physical harm to a puppy or to a person nearby. For these types of actions, your puppy should be punished using the same word and action every time. Your puppy should not be rewarded or be allowed to participate in fun playtime for at least ten to fifteen minutes after the incident and punishment.

If your puppy is in the house with several family members, it is important that everyone show their disapproval of the action. If one family member disciplines the puppy and another one starts playing with him immediately after the punishment, the puppy may become confused and it may take longer to stop the unwanted behavior. Dog owners need to be aware that not all dogs learn at the same rate, and that some puppies may be punished for weeks or months for the same action until they learn to stop that action completely.

When Not to Punish a Puppy

If a puppy's actions do not harm anyone, he probably doesn't need to be punished. Words like "no" or "stop" could still be used to signal disapproval of the action. It is important to not punish a puppy for not learning tricks or for not picking up on training fast enough. If a new dog owner spends several hours a day training, positively reinforcing, and nurturing good behavior, the amount of negative behavior will lessen and could possibly lead to fewer situations requiring punishment.

Proactive training and reinforcement of good behavior is usually more effective than constant reactive punishment. Dogs generally want to please their owners and in return be given attention and love.

The Most Difficult Situations

One of the more difficult training parts is teaching a puppy to stay put until called to come to its owner. If your puppy breaks its stay and runs off, it is important to not chase after your puppy and reward it with lots of attention when it returns. If the puppy runs, is caught, or returns and is disciplined negatively, your puppy will associate discipline with coming to its owner. Training your puppy to come will then become more difficult.

When teaching the *stay* and *come* command, it is important to do so in a closed or fenced area so that the puppy will not run into the street or into an area where it might get hurt.

If an owner puts his or her dog in an area that could cause danger, it is unfair to punish the dog.

If a puppy is constantly misbehaving and nothing seems to be working, puppy training classes with other dogs and dog owners may be a solution.

Realistic expectations of a puppy's behavior and actions are crucial. It takes many breeds months to completely learn what is expected of them-household routines and rules as well as basic manners. Puppy owners need to be patient, remain consistent in their training and punishment procedures, and remember that as each month passes their puppy becomes a little bit bigger, a little more mature and little better behaved. Before you know it, you'll have a well-mannered companion that you'll wonder how you ever lived without.

MEET THE AUTHOR

Amy & 8-Month-Old Cozmo

Amy Morford has over twenty years of dog training experience with companion dogs, sport dogs and working breeds. Amy's motivation to write about dogs stems from her love for them and their unbiased loyalty and devotion. Amy's goal is to provide helpful, accurate information to assist dog lovers with raising and training a well-mannered, good-tempered, happy, healthy, well-adjusted companion, friend, partner and/or family pet.

Be sure to bookmark and subscribe to *DogTrainingPlace.Net* for articles, tips and tail wagging fun.

OTHER BOOKS AND PRODUCTS BY AMY

DoggyPedia: All You Need To Know About Dogs

Dog Eldercare: Caring For Your Middle-Aged To Older Dog

Dog Quotes: Proverbs, Quotes & Quips

How To Speak Dog: Dog Training Simplified For Dog Owners

Pet Names and Numerology: Choose the Right Name For Your Pet

Scared Dog Audio

The German Shepherd Big Book: All About The German Shepherd Breed